Hair Today, Gone Tomorrow

A Readers' Theater Script and Guide

By Nancy K. Wallace • Illustrated by Michelle Henninger

magic wagon

visit us at www.abdopublishing.com

To my daughters, Mollie and Elizabeth, who have spent endless hours helping with library plays! —NKW

Printed in the United States of America, North Mankato, Minnesota.
042013
092013
 This book contains at least 10% recycled materials.

Written by Nancy K. Wallace
Illustrations by Michelle Henninger
Edited by Stephanie Hedlund and Rochelle Baltzer
Cover and interior design by Renée LaViolette

Library of Congress Cataloging-in-Publication Data
Wallace, Nancy K.
  Hair today, gone tomorrow : a readers' theater script and guide / written by Nancy K. Wallace ; illustrated by Michelle Henninger.
     pages cm. -- (Readers' theater: how to put on a production)
  ISBN 978-1-61641-986-8
1. Rapunzel (Tale)--Adaptations--Juvenile drama. 2. Fairy tales--Adaptations--Juvenile drama. 3. Theater--Production and direction--Juvenile literature. 4. Readers' theater--Juvenile literature. I. Henninger, Michelle. II. Title.
  PS3623.A4436H35 2013
  812'.6--dc23
                    2013011504

Table of Contents

School Plays

Do you like to make props, paint scenery, or act on stage? You should put on a production. Plays are lots of fun! And a play is a great way for kids to work together as a team!

A readers' theater production can be done by just reading your lines. You don't have to memorize them! An adapted readers' theater production looks more like a regular play. The performers wear makeup and costumes. The stage has scenery and props. The cast moves around to show the action. But, performers can still read their scripts.

To hold a production, you will need a large space. An auditorium with a stage is ideal. A classroom will work, too. Now, choose a date and get permission to use the space.

You'll need tickets that list important information. Your production can also have a playbill. It is a printed program. Playbills list all of the cast and production team inside.

Finally, make flyers or posters to advertise your play. Place them around your school and community. Tell your friends and family. Everyone enjoys watching kids perform!

Cast & Crew

There are many people needed to put on a production. First, decide who will play each part. Each person in the cast will need a script. All the performers should practice their lines.

Hair Today, Gone Tomorrow has a lot of speaking parts.

> Queen - Rapunzel's mother
>
> Rapunzel - Our heroine
>
> Bartholomew - The page
>
> Meg - Rapunzel's best friend
>
> Student 1 - Student at Rapunzel's school
>
> Student 2 - Student at Rapunzel's school
>
> Additional students are needed for nonspeaking parts in scene two.

Next, a crew is needed. The show can't go on without these important people! Some jobs can be combined. Every show needs a director. This person organizes everything and everyone in the show.

The director works with the production crew. This includes the costume designers, who borrow or make all the costumes. Stage managers make sure things run smoothly. Sometimes they even have assistant stage managers.

Your production can also have a stage crew. This includes lighting designers to run spotlights and other lighting. Set designers plan and make scenery.

The special effects crew takes care of sound and other unusual effects. In *Hair Today, Gone Tomorrow*, they need to make a crashing sound as Bartholomew knocks over a potted plant. They also need to make the sound of horses whinnying and hooves stomping as the coach leaves.

Sets & Props

At a readers' theater production, the performers sit on stools at the front of the room. But, an adapted readers' theater production or full play requires some sets and props.

Sets include a background for each scene of the play. *Hair Today, Gone Tomorrow* could have the following scene sets:

Scene 1 is in a castle. Paint sheets of cardboard to look like a stone wall. Cut out the front of a large box to make a fireplace and paint it to look like stones. Put real logs inside it.

Scene 2 is in a school. Make posters to hang on the walls and paint lockers on large sheets of cardboard.

Scene 3 & 4 are in Rapunzel's bedroom. The stone wall from Scene 1 can be used here, too. Get a real bed or use two chairs for the girls to sit on. Scene 5 takes place in the castle garden. Reuse the stone wall from Scene 1. Place real or fake plants around to make it look like a garden.

Props are things you'll need during the play. *Hair Today, Gone Tomorrow* could have the following props:

A banner or sign to hang over the fireplace that says: "The Kingdom of Happily Ever After." Make a cone hat for Rapunzel out of cardboard covered with felt. Punch two holes near the bottom edge to attach the braids with a single strand of yarn. Attach strands of yarn braided into fourteen-foot braids.

Rapunzel's page uses a different colored pillow for her hair each day. The script has red, green, gold, and lavender. You can cover the same pillow with different pillow cases or adjust the script to match pillows you already have. The students in Scene 2 need books or backpacks to carry. Hang a large mirror on the wall in Rapunzel's bedroom for Scenes 3 & 4.

Makeup & Costumes

The stage and props aren't the only things people will be looking at in your play! The makeup artist has a big job. Stage makeup needs to be brighter than regular makeup. Even boys wear stage makeup!

Costume designers set the scene just as much as set designers. They borrow costumes or adapt old clothing for each character. For example, make a cloak out of a length of fabric gathered at the neck. Ask adults if you need help finding or sewing costumes.

Hair Today, Gone Tomorrow performers will need these costumes:

> Queen - A long, fancy dress with a large crown
>
> Rapunzel - A long, fancy dress with a small crown and the hat with braids
>
> Bartholomew - A floppy beret with a feather and a tunic with tights or leggings
>
> Meg, Student 1, Student 2, and additional nonspeaking students - Current school clothes

Stage Directions

When your sets, props, and costumes are ready, it is important to rehearse. Choose a time that everyone can attend. Try to have at least five or six rehearsals before your show.

You should practice together as a team even if you will be reading your scripts for readers' theater. A play should sound like a conversation. Try to avoid pauses when no one is speaking. You can do this by adding sound effects.

Some theater terms may seem strange. The wings are the sides of the stage that the audience can't see. The house is where the audience sits. The curtains refers to the main curtain at the front of the stage.

When reading your script, the stage directions are in parentheses. They are given from the performer's point of view. You will be facing the audience when you are performing. Left will be on your left and right will be on your right. When rehearsing, perform the stage directions and the lines to get used to moving around the stage.

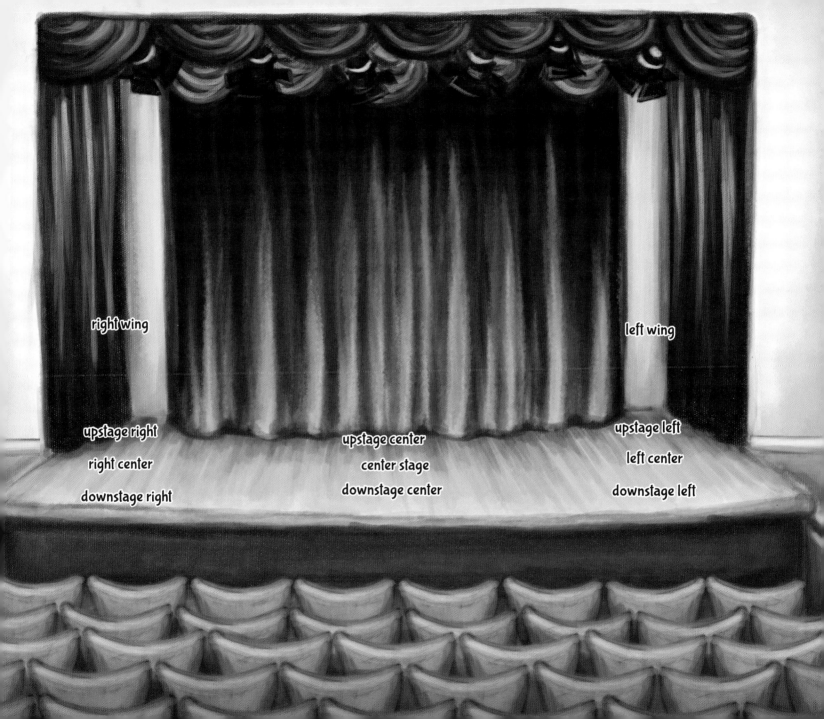

Script: Hair Today, Gone Tomorrow

(Opening of the curtain for scene 1 — The Castle. A sign or banner saying: "The Kingdom of Happily Ever After" hangs over the painted cardboard fireplace at center stage. The queen stands at stage right.)

Queen: *(Putting her hands to her mouth to call out)* Rapunzel! You're going to be late for school again!

(Rapunzel walks on from stage left. A member of the stage crew holds one long braid in the wings as though it is snagged offstage.)

Rapunzel: I'm coming, Mother! My hair is stuck! *(She pulls on her braid with both hands and yanks it loose.)*

Queen: Where is your page, darling?

Rapunzel: *You* sent Bartholomew downstairs to get a different colored pillow for my hair.

Queen: Oh yes, the one he had was quite inappropriate! He had a red pillow. And Monday's pillow is red. Today is Tuesday, so the pillow should be green.

Rapunzel: *(Rolling her eyes)* What possible difference could it make?

Queen: It's tradition, darling. Just as it is tradition that princesses cannot cut their hair until after they are married.

Rapunzel: I wonder if that will ever happen!

Queen: *(Smiling)* This is the Kingdom of Happily Ever After, my darling. We specialize in happy endings.

Rapunzel: How am I going to attract a prince? I am the only princess in the twenty-first century that still dresses as though I were living in medieval times!

Queen: That's not true, darling. Princess Anne of Once Upon a Time still dresses traditionally, too.

Rapunzel: But, she's 150 years old and she's still single! Obviously, men didn't line up to marry her, either.

Queen: Now, now, dear, don't you worry. Next year we'll have a magnificent ball for your sixteenth birthday. I'll invite all the eligible princes. They won't be able to take their eyes off you and your beautiful hair.

Rapunzel: Just how many eligible princes are there anyway?

Queen: *(Counting on her fingers)* At least five. I'll have to check.

Rapunzel: There is a really cute boy named Michael in my English class. He asked me if I wanted to get pizza on Friday.

Queen: Tell him no, dear. He's not of royal blood. It would be completely inappropriate.

(Rapunzel looks disgusted and turns away. Bartholomew runs in from stage left.)

Bartholomew: Your Majesties, I am sorry to have detained you. I have the correct pillow now.

(He arranges Rapunzel's hair on the pillow in a circle and then follows behind her wherever she walks, to carry her hair.)

Queen: Run along, dear! Your coach is waiting. I'll see you after school!

Rapunzel: Oh great, now I'm off to school in my coach with six white horses! Why can't I ride the school bus like everybody else? *(Exits stage left with page behind her)*

(Curtain opens on scene 2 — The School. Students are clustered in small groups walking along the hall from both directions. They turn, giggling and pointing as Rapunzel walks in from stage left.)

Bartholomew: Her Royal Majesty, Princess Rapunzel, of the Kingdom of Happily Ever After!

Student 1: *(Giggling)* They should call it the Kingdom of Hair Ever After.

Student 2: Or how about The Braidy Bunch?

Rapunzel: *(Whispers)* Bartholomew, please don't announce me at school! It's embarrassing.

Bartholomew: But your mother insists . . .

Rapunzel: My mother isn't here. It's hard enough being the only one who is different. Cut the title, please!

(Meg is waiting and runs over to meet Rapunzel.)

Meg: The bell just rang! We'd better hurry! Why are you late?

Rapunzel: Oh, Mother was all upset because Bartholomew had Monday's pillow instead of today's.

Meg: What difference would it make?

Rapunzel: That's just what I said. Apparently, the Kingdom of Happily Ever After will fall apart if tradition isn't followed to the letter.

Meg: Maybe the kingdom needs to fall apart. Change is a good thing.

Rapunzel: Would you tell my mother that?

Meg: (Shaking her head) Ahh, I'd rather not. She isn't usually open to suggestions. Come on. We need to hurry. We have gym first period.

Rapunzel: Oh great! Bartholomew, I hope you can run laps with my hair on that pillow.

Bartholomew: I will do my best, Your Majesty! Just warn me before you speed up!

(Meg and Rapunzel rush off stage right as Bartholomew follows behind.)

(Curtain opens on scene 3 — Rapunzel's Bedroom. The girls sit on a bed or two chairs.)

Meg: I saw Michael talking to you after gym. What did he say?

Rapunzel: He asked me again about having pizza Friday night.

Meg: Did you tell him yes?

Rapunzel: Not yet. I told him I had to check my social calendar.

Meg: *(Giggling)* I didn't know you had one.

Rapunzel: I don't. But Michael doesn't know that. Besides, my mother says I can't have pizza with him because he's not of royal blood.

Meg: Rapunzel, ninety-nine percent of the world isn't of royal blood!

Rapunzel: I'm tired of being a princess. And I'm *so* tired of all this hair! Last night, I dreamed I was being attacked by boa constrictors. I woke up to find I was tangled in my braids!

Meg: *(Giggling)* That's kind of funny.

Rapunzel: It's not funny. It's scary. Do you know how hard it is to even take a shower? And last week, I went riding and Bartholomew put my hair in a velvet sack. It bounced on the horse's behind and scared him. He raced into the Magic Forest and I almost fell off.

Meg: You're right. That's not funny.

Rapunzel: I have to do something! I can't live like this.

Meg: I have a suggestion if you're brave enough to try it.

Rapunzel: What?

Meg: (*Holds up a pair of scissors and snips the air with them*) Let's cut your hair!

(*Scene 4 — Rapunzel's Bedroom a few minutes later*)

Meg: Are you absolutely sure? If I do this, I don't want you to be mad at me for talking you into it.

Rapunzel: I'm sure, Meg. I just wish there was some way we could do it so my mom wouldn't know about it right away. Maybe I can convince her that breaking tradition isn't such a bad thing.

Meg: (Stands back and takes hold of one braid) Well, I had an idea about that, too. If we just cut off your braids, we can reattach them to your cone hat. As long as you wear your hat, she'll never know.

Rapunzel: You're a genius! Let's do it.

Meg: Okay, here goes! (She carefully snips the yarn attaching one braid to the hat and hands it to Rapunzel.)

Rapunzel: This isn't even pretty! It looks like a big ugly rope! Cut the other one off, too!

(Meg snips off the other braid and gives it to Rapunzel. Rapunzel reaches up to take off her cone hat.)

Meg: Wait! Wait! Come over here in front of the mirror!

Rapunzel: My head feels so much lighter. I'm almost afraid to see what I look like. (She pulls the cone hat off and throws it on the floor.)

(Meg stands behind her and fluffs up her hair.)

Meg: Look how cute your hair is! You look beautiful!

Rapunzel: I love my hair! Thank you so much, Meg! You are the best friend ever! (She hugs Meg.)

Meg: Now, let's get these braids tied back on the hat before we have any unexpected visitors.

(*Curtain opens on Scene 5 — The Castle Garden. Set scene with fake stone wall and potted plants. Queen stands at stage right. Cue sound effects for the coach arriving off stage.*)

Queen: Finally, here she comes! We have guests arriving for a Royal Tea Party in half an hour. I want my little darling to look her best!

Bartholomew: (*Walks on from stage left carrying a gold pillow*) Good afternoon, Your Majesty!

Queen: What are you doing with that pillow, Bartholomew? This is Thursday! Thursday's pillow is lavender!

Bartholomew: My apologies, Your Majesty. I will get the appropriate pillow at once.

Queen: My goodness, I should hope so! Perhaps I need to hire a new page!

Bartholomew: I promise to do better in the future, Your Majesty.

Rapunzel: (Enters stage left with her braids looped over her arm. One braid extends off stage) I spilled milk on the lavender pillow at breakfast, Mother. It wasn't Bartholomew's fault that we had to use the gold one.

Queen: Oh, I see. My apologies, Bartholomew. Perhaps the lavender pillow has been laundered by now. Go and see.

Bartholomew: Yes, Your Majesty.

Queen: Hello, my dearest darling! Hello, Meg!

Meg: Good afternoon, Your Majesty!

Rapunzel: *(Looks at Meg and then at her mother)* Mother, can we talk? Maybe we don't need the lavender pillow after all.

(Page backs off to exit stage right. He bumps into a potted plant and knocks it over on his way off stage. Sound Effects: a crash followed by horses whinnying and hooves clomping off stage.)

Rapunzel: *(Grabbing her cone hat with both hands and acting as though she is being yanked offstage)* My hair is stuck in the coach door!

Queen: *(Running to help her)* Oh, my poor darling!

Meg: Rapunzel, you'll be dragged by the coach! Let your hat go!

Rapunzel: *(Crying)* Oh no!

(She lets her hat go and it is dragged offstage by the unseen stage crew. She puts her hands over her face.)

Queen: *(Throws her arms around Rapunzel and touches her hair)* Oh, my poor darling. You cut your hair.

Meg: No, I cut it.

Rapunzel: But I asked her to, Mother.

Queen: *(Patting Rapunzel's head)* I'm so thankful that you did. You could have been killed. All because of those terrible braids!

Rapunzel: *(Sounding surprised)* Terrible braids?

Queen: I didn't tell you, but I hated my braids, too. The first thing I did after I married your father was cut my hair!

Rapunzel: You did?!

Queen: It's a ridiculous tradition! And so is riding to school in a coach. I'll call the school and ask the bus to pick you up tomorrow.

Rapunzel: Wow, thank you! What made you change your mind?

Queen: Almost having my daughter dragged through the courtyard by her hair! Suddenly, tradition doesn't seem very important anymore. *(Putting an arm around Meg and Rapunzel)* Come on, girls. We're going to be late for tea.

Rapunzel: Since you are in such a good mood, is there any chance I could have pizza with Michael on Friday night?

Queen: Oh, why not? He's a nice boy isn't he?

Meg and Rapunzel *(Together)*: Very nice!

Queen: Just remember to be home by twelve, because, well, it's tradition . . .

Rapunzel: *(Laughing)* I know. It's tradition for coaches to turn into pumpkins at midnight!

The End

Adapting Readers' Theater Scripts

Readers' theater can be done very simply. You just read your lines. You don't have to memorize them! Performers sit on chairs or stools. They read their parts without moving around.

Adapted Readers' Theater

This looks more like a regular play. The performers wear makeup and costumes. The stage has scenery and props. The cast moves around to show the action. Performers can still read their scripts.

Hold a Puppet Show

Some schools and libraries have puppet collections. Students make the puppets be the actors. They read their scripts.

Teacher's Guides

Readers' Theater Teacher's Guides are available online. Each guide includes reading levels for each character and additional production tips for each play. Visit Teacher's Guides at **www.abdopublishing.com** to get yours today!